COSTUME & FASHION

COSTUME & FASHION

DOVERPICTURA

DOVER PUBLICATIONS, INC. | Mineola, New York

By Alan Weller.
Designed by Joel Waldrep and Megan Herndon.

Costume & Fashion is a new work, first published by Dover Publications, Inc.,
in 2009.

For permission to use more than ten images, please contact:
Permissions Department
Dover Publications, Inc.
31 East 2nd Street
Mineola, NY 11501
rights@doverpublications.com

The CD-ROM file names correspond to the images in the book. All of the artwork
stored on the CD-ROM can be imported directly into a wide range of design and
word-processing programs on either Windows or Macintosh platforms. No further
installation is necessary.

ISBN 10: 0-486-99046-X
ISBN 13: 978-0-486-99046-0
Manufactured in the United States of America
Dover Publications, Inc., 31 East 2nd Street, Mineola, NY 11501
www.doverpublications.com

005

009

010

011

013

014

015

016

017

019

020

022

025

027

028

029

030

031 background

032

033

034

035

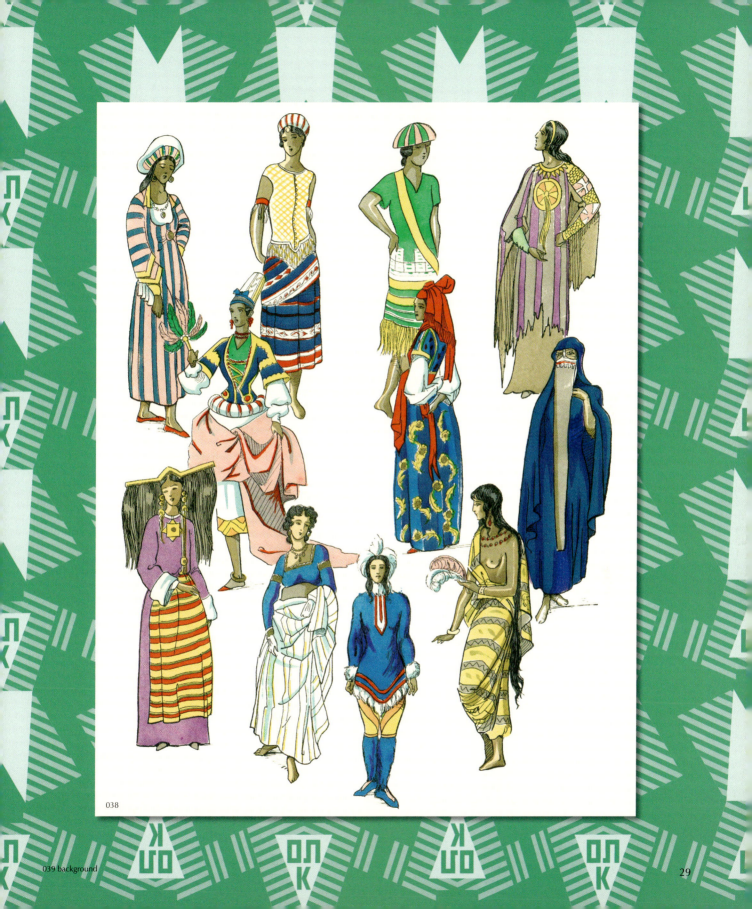

041

043

044

33

045

046

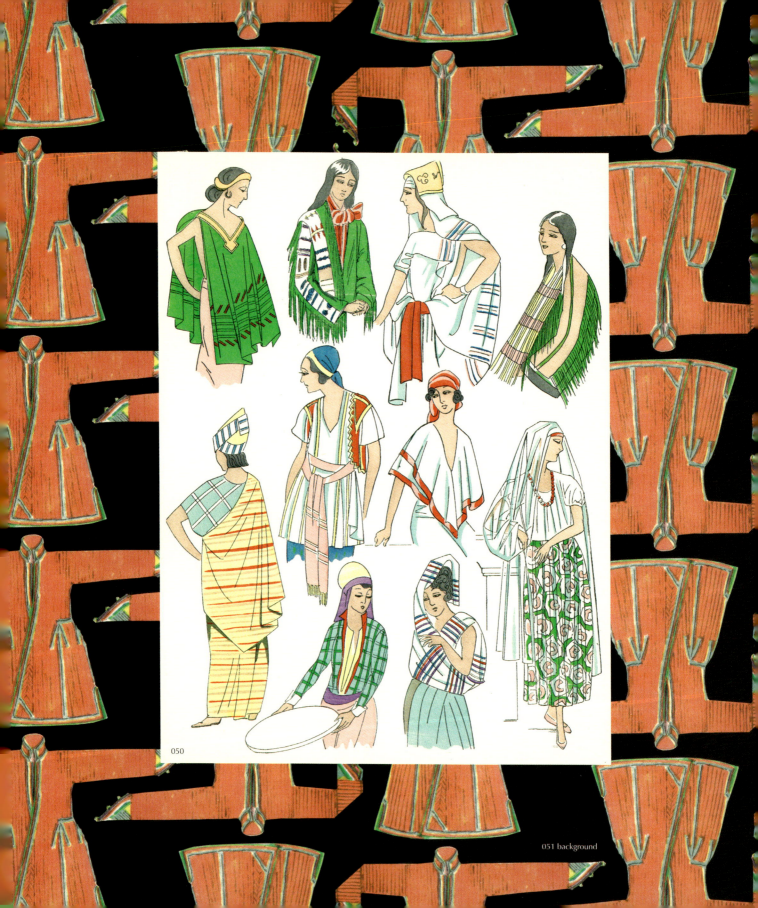

050

052

053   054   055

057

058

41

059

060

061

063

065

066

067

068

069

070

071

MCMXXI

GEORGE BA

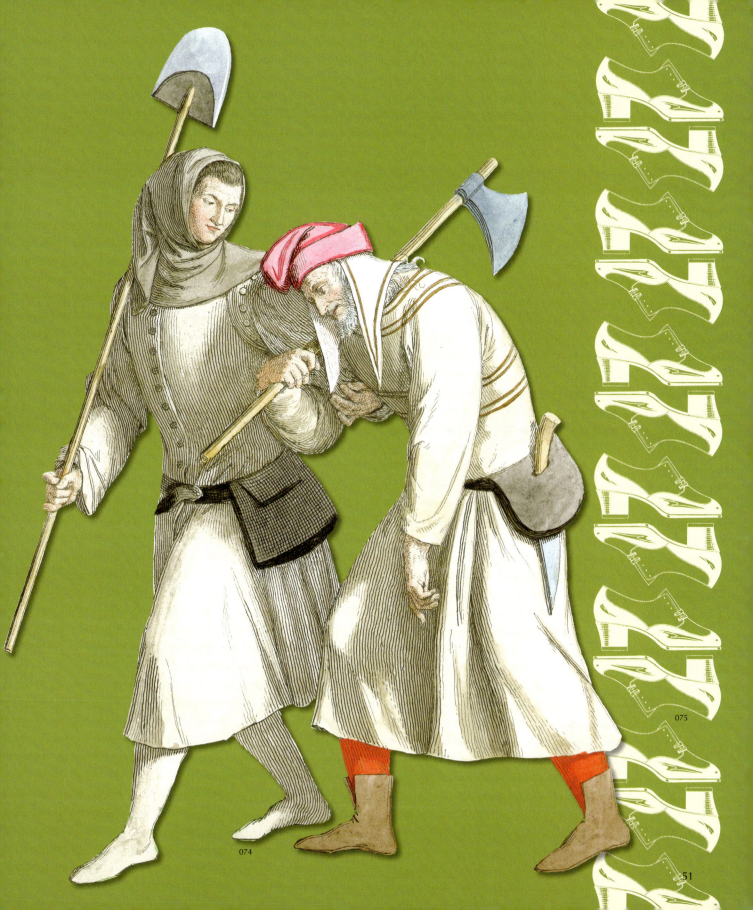

074

075

076

079

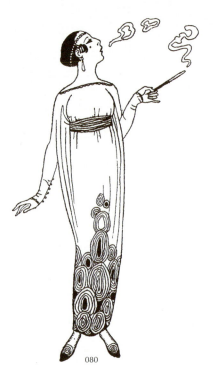

080

081

082

083

084

085

086

088

089

091

092

093

094

096

097

098

099

102

104

106

107

108

109

74

110

111

112

113

114

115

116

118

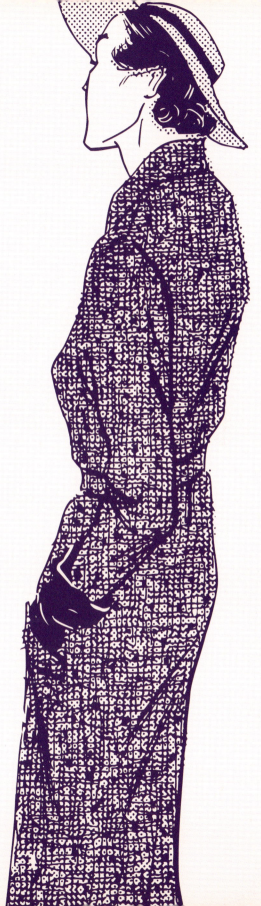

119

120

121

122

123

124

125

126

127

132

133

134

135

137

136

139

141

142

92

143

144

145

146

147

148

150

151

152

153

154

155

156

158

159

162

163

164

166

167

168

169

109

170

171

172

173

176

177

112

178

179

180

181

182

184

185

186

187

188

189

190

117

118

191

192

193

119

195

196

194

197

198

199

202

203

205

206

List of Images

List of Vector Images